Customer Service Training For Front Line Personnel

By

The Customer Service
Training Institute

Other Customer Service Training Manuals from
The Customer Service Training Institute

Customer Service Basics

Service Recovery Skills

How to Interact with All Kinds of Customers

Great Customer Service Over the Phone

Enhancing the Customer Experience

Customer Service Training for Managers & Supervisors

Customer Service Training for Service Technicians

Customer Service Training for the Hospitality Sector

Customer Service Training for Health Care Professionals

Customer Service Excellence for Security Officers

Safety in the Workplace

"Those employees who are among the first to meet our customers are the most important employees we have."

Table of Contents

Introduction

It is usually thought that the future of any business lies mainly with the management of the company. Decisions made at the upper management level decide the direction that the company will take in the future. These decisions take into consideration things like market share, company resources, marketing trends, and other fiscal and logistic items. These decisions may involve millions, or billions, of dollars!

There is another train of thought that we will discuss in these pages. That is: **The people that deal directly with the customers on a daily basis determine the future of any business!**

Take a moment and think about this concept. Who do your customers deal with when they purchase goods or services from your company? The vast majority of customers will never see, talk, or correspond with senior management. They deal with front-line service people!

If front-line people do their job properly and effectively, they can become the single most important asset of a company. Individuals that perfect their customer service skills become more valuable in the marketplace and command larger salaries than their unskilled counterparts! They also have more opportunities open to them.

We will discuss the importance of the initial contact your customers have with you or your company. We will explain why this contact will often shape the entire perception your customers have about you! We will also discuss how you can help your customers develop an extremely positive image of you and your company.

Who Are Front-Line Service People?

The term "Front-Line Service" refers to the group of employees or individuals that have direct contact with your customers on a daily basis. This would include, but not be limited to, cashiers, clerks, salespeople, order takers, bank tellers, delivery people, etc.

These are the people that determine whether the customer has a positive or negative experience when they do business with the company. If the experience is positive, customers will tend to come back. If the experience is negative, it is likely that your customer will go elsewhere next time. Unless a company is the only source for a specific product or service, customers will continue to patronize the business that makes them feel wanted and appreciated.

Front-Line people are the people who represent the company and project the image that the customers receive about that company.

That is why this group of people must be given the skills and training to prepare them to deal effectively with customers on a daily basis!

If you were in the army, you would not think even think about sending a group of soldiers into combat without the proper training. Yet every day businesses are allowing their front-line employees to service their customers without providing any Customer Service training! Customer Service training allows people to become more effective and represent the business in the most effective manner. Without the proper training, you could be sending your customers the wrong message.

In the pages that follow we will be giving you the basic skills you will need to be effective as a front-line employee. The material is designed to make you think. We will provide you with the basic tools you need and give you ideas on how to implement them. It is up to you to practice and develop these skills until they become habit.

What Makes Customers Come Back?

Front line service people control the customer's experience during the time they deal with the company. From the time they walk through the door or pick up the phone, front line service people control how the customer will view the entire company.

Take a moment and think about how you judge or critique things in your own life. If something makes you feel good, you tend to associate a positive image to that experience. You will tend to want to repeat that experience over and over again. On the other hand, if an experience makes you feel bad or uncomfortable, you will associate a negative image to the experience. You will then tend to avoid repeating the experience because you want to avoid anything associated with pain or discomfort.

In order to create a positive experience for your customers, you first need to understand what your customers are looking for.

Your understanding of exactly what your customers expect enables you to design an effective strategy for providing exceptional customer service.

Making Customers Feel Appreciated

Perhaps the single most important thing any business can do is to make their customers feel important and appreciated. The more your customers feel appreciated and wanted, the greater chance you have that they will come back again to patronize your business. Why is this?

The vast majority of us work for a living. We work to earn money to pay for our homes, put food on the table, and to enable us to have a certain lifestyle. We work hard for our money. The harder we work for something, the higher value we place on it. Because of this, people tend to want to give their money to a person or business that makes them feel appreciated and valuable. How do you give your customers that feeling?

People react to the way they are treated. Generally, people will place a great deal of importance on a first impression.

If that first impression is favorable, they will tend to be open-minded and receptive to the rest of the experience. If the first impression is negative, they may terminate the experience immediately, giving you and your company no opportunity to recover.

Knowing the Value of your Customers!

It is easy to underestimate the value of a customer. This is especially true in businesses where the amount of the average purchase is just a few dollars. As we underestimate a customer's value, we tend to minimize the need to take steps to make these customers happy.

Our minds treat things according to the value we place on them. We are more apt to take good care on an expensive item than we are a cheap, throw away piece. Think for a moment. If you were offered $20.00 to do a job, you may feel it is not worth the time or inconvenience involved. If that same job paid $1000.00, you would think a little bit more about your decision. The same goes for your customers.

It is important that you realize just how much each of your customers is worth to your business.

When you can accurately understand their value, you will find yourself treating them very differently.

A very common misconception is that the value of each customer is equal to the amount of his or her last purchase. For example, if a customer buys a quart of milk from you for $2.00, then the value of that customer is $2.00. In reality, the value of that customer is far greater.

When we talk about the value of a customer, we must take into consideration the amount of purchases, the frequency of purchases, and the anticipated amount of time that customer will make those purchases. After taking all these factors into consideration, we can arrive at the true value of that customer. Below are a few examples:

1) A customer buys a quart of milk for $2.00 twice a week. The value of that customer should be $4.00 per week, $208 per year, or $2080 over 10 years!

If you do something to anger that customer, the loss to your company over time would be over $2000!

2) A customer buys a copy machine for $500.00 and a one-year service contract for $200.00. The average life of the copier is 7 years. The cost of 7 years of service contracts is $1400.00. The copier will also use supplies worth $250.00 per year.

The cost of supplies over 7 years will be $1750.00. Therefore, this customers worth to your company would be $500 + $1400 + 1750 or $3650!

These figures do not include two very important factors that cannot be accurately measured. Those two factors are the amount of additional business or purchases over and above their normal purchases, and the amount of referral business that they are responsible for.

Referral business is additional business that is generated by the positive comments or recommendation made by your customer. For example, a current customer recommends your business to a few of his friends that he knows are in the market for your product or service. This referral will only occur if your customer is happy with your business.

The amount of referral business can be staggering. You never know whom your customers will be talking to about your company. One recommendation can be worth thousands of dollars in business! Good news also travels fast. One person tells another, who tells another, etc. Though it is impossible to trace future business back to an original referral, it is not uncommon to have referral business that far outweighs what your original customer may purchase themselves from your business! Here are a few examples:

1)   A person buys a roast beef sandwich for lunch at a local deli. The meat on the sandwich is of very poor quality. The person returns to the deli and asks for a new sandwich. The deli refuses. The cost to make the sandwich is $2.00. What can the bad sandwich cost the deli in the long run?

Let's say the average person buys lunch out twice a week and spends an average of $5.00 per lunch. That's $10.00 per week or $500.00 per year. This same customer works in an office with several other people. Let's say he tells two of his co-workers about the experience. They do not wish to get the same kind of treatment so they go to another deli for their lunch. Two people at $500.00 per year equals $1,000.00. The office also caters ten business lunches a year. Each lunch costs them $250.00. The quality of the food is important so, after hearing of the bad experience, they choose another business to cater the lunches. The amount of this business $2,500.00. The total loss of business would be $4,000.00! Four thousand dollars of lost business because of a sandwich that costs $2.00 to make!

2)   Mr. Hubbard attends a local business club luncheon at a local conference center. His food arrives and it is barely warm. He asks the waiter to take the food back and heat it up. The waiter takes the food, and instead of re-heating it, prepares an entire new entree and serves it to Mr. Hubbard along with an apology. The waiter also returns a few minutes later to make sure the new entree is satisfactory.

A few months later, Mr. Hubbard's company is considering potential locations to hold their national meeting. He remembers the excellent treatment he received from the waiter at the convention center and recommends that location. The convention center gets the week-long meeting along with the over $30,000 in business it generates. The convention center gets this meeting for the next 5 years. Total business generated, $150,000! Cost of satisfying the customer? An entree and a few words.

The above two examples are conservative in nature. They are designed to demonstrate just how much money and business may possibly be won or lost depending on how you treat a customer.

In addition, note who was involved in both examples. A deli clerk and a waiter. Front line people! No one in management was responsible for either customer experience! These two examples clearly show the power and influence front line service people can have in business!

Never Under-Estimate the Value of a Customer!

All businesses have certain customers that are treated differently than the rest. The customers buy large amounts of product or maybe recommend your products or services to their clients. Their purchases or recommendations represent considerable business for your company. When these customers want something, you tend to do everything in your power to accommodate them.

In the building trades, these customers may be large developers. In retail business, it may be a large chain of stores. In a specialized industry it may be one company that purchases all of your product! (Like the company that sells McDonalds it's french fries!)

Whatever the situation, you tend to do whatever you fell is necessary to insure that your company retains their business.

That's only common sense. Here's something to think about, however.

When the next customer walks through your door, how do you know his or her importance?

In the second example you just read, the gentleman with the bad entree did not give any clue to the waiter as to his job or of a possible referral for future business. He was just an ordinary man with a problem. A problem that just happened to be solved in an exceptional manner.

There will be many instances where you will come into contact with customers that could have a considerable influence over those people that deal with your company. It is not possible for you to know who all these people are. You may know who an important client is but do you know what his or her spouse looks like? We all know what our boss looks like but how many of us know what our bosses parents look like? If we did, I'm sure that we would treat them just a little bit differently, wouldn't we?

The point that I am trying to make is that we should establish a minimum level of service that we provide to every customer that walks through the door. That minimum level of service should be at a level where no one could feel that he or she was not considered important to your company.

As previously stated, our minds tend to treat people and situations according to the value we place on them.

If we learn to view every customer as a potential referral for a major new account, you will find yourself treating all your customers just a little bit better.

The Importance of the First Contact

In any business, the first contact with a customer should be made in a friendly and helpful manner. A warm greeting followed by a "How can I help You" will often be perceived as a positive greeting. It is important that the customer be put at ease and is aware of your sincere desire to help them. Very often customers will feel awkward when asking for help and may even leave without asking for assistance if they cannot find the product they need.

In some businesses, it may not be possible to personally greet every customer that walks through the door. The volume may be just too much or there may be many entrances to the particular location.

In cases like these, every effort should be made to make assistance readily available to the customer.

This can be accomplished through the use of roving salespeople, managers, or even greeters.

Greeters are employees whose only function is to greet customers as they enter the store. Usually, greeters are stationed at the entrances of the store and will greet every customer as they come through the door. In some cases, such as warehouse club stores, the greeters will ask to see membership cards. The greeter then performs two important tasks; they allow only members into the store and also greet each customer and provide information when asked.

You may be asking yourself if the expense and added "work" involved in greeting customers is worthwhile. In the course of this publication you will see this phrase repeated several times: "Never give a customer a reason to shop anywhere else. A customer that goes to your competition is a customer you may never see again!"

Let's stop for a minute and think about that statement. If one of your customers should go into your competition for any reason, what may happen? That customer is going to get a first hand look at your competition and what they have to offer. They will compare you against them and make a conscious or sub-conscious decision as to where they will continue to shop in the future. Once in the competition's store, they will also be subjected to the employees of that store and their efforts to grab a new customer.

If this experience is more favorable than the last experience the customer had in your store, where do you think that customer will shop in the future? Right, the competition. Not only have you lost a customer, your competition has also gained one.

Important: While it is nice to be greeted when you enter an establishment, customers will tend to be "turned off" if they are constantly asked if they need assistance or feel "bombarded" by constant attention from employees. A good rule of thumb is to greet a customer once and then approach him or her only if they look like they need assistance. If the customer has a puzzled look on their face, or if you see them walking around the same part of the store over and over again looking for something, then offer assistance. Otherwise, leave them alone. Remember your goal is to make them feel at ease in your store.

Making It Easy on the Customer

What do you think the term "Customer Friendly" means? The term "Customer Friendly" means creating an environment that your customers will enjoy when they patronize your store.

Let's say you had to purchase a specific item. You have two choices of where you can get the item. **Store A** makes you find the item on the shelf, get the number, stand on line to order it, stand on another line to pay for it, and then stand on a third line to pick it up. **Store B** lets you get the item off the shelf, take it to one of many cashiers and you're on your way. **Store B** also will load you package in your car if it's heavy, **Store A** gives you string to tie it down but you must load it yourself.

Which store is more "Customer Friendly"? Store B of course. Store B makes it easier for their customers to get what they want and get out fast!

They assist their customers in loading and securing large items! They make it easy for the customer to do business with them.

On another level, Store B makes itself appealing to a wider segment of the population. How? Think about it. Let's say you are an older person that wants to purchase something that's a little heavy such as a lawn mower or barbecue grille. Where do you think you would go to make your purchase? You can't load the unit yourself so Store B would be an easy choice.

In order for a business to grow in this economy, it must make itself attractive to the population around it. A successful business focuses on what it can do to make the shopping experience as easy as possible for the customer.

The same reasoning is used when stores provide play areas for small children. These businesses realize the benefits of having these areas. They know that parents are more likely to go someplace where their children can be occupied than someplace where the children will be unhappy and frustrated. A perfect example of this is fast food restaurants. Do you think that these restaurants paid thousands of dollars for play equipment out of the goodness of their hearts? Of course not! They realize that Mom and Dad are going to eat there because they can get a little peace and quiet while the kids play!

When it comes to Customer Service skills, an employee should determine what it is that he or she can do to make it easy for the customer to do business with their company.

The following are examples of what can be done to make a business more customer friendly:

1) **Assist the customer as much as possible.**

If a customer asks you where the widgets are, don't just say "Aisle 3, on the left", walk the customer over to where the product is. Then offer your assistance on choosing the proper product. In instances where there are several different types, sizes, or brands to choose from, your input may be the difference between a happy customer and a dissatisfied customer.

2) **Streamline the purchase process.**

Generally speaking, the fewer the number of steps required to make a purchase, the happier the customer will be. For example, picking a product off the shelf, paying for it, and leaving is much easier on the customer than standing on a line to order, another line to pay, and yet another line to pick it up. The faster the customer can get through the process the happier they will be.

3) **Keep wait time to a minimum.**

If there is one thing people hate, it's waiting on line. Make sure you have adequate facilities to handle the customer traffic during the busiest time of the day.

Schedule people in accordance with customer traffic demands. Have more cashiers open during busy times to reduce lines.

Wait time is extremely important if your type of business involves items that must be purchased regularly or at the spur of the moment. For example, if you sell milk or bread, you don't want people to purchase somewhere else because your store always has long lines. People on their lunch hour or on their way home from work cannot be kept waiting on line.

Wait time is part of the purchase process. As previously stated, the faster the customer can get through the process, the happier they will become.

4) Make things easy to find.

A well laid out store or catalog will speed up the shopping process considerably. A poorly laid out store will lead to frustration and will eventually cost you in lost customers. Have maps of the floor layout readily available.

5) Make it easy to get assistance.

Every employee should make it a priority to assist customers. If you see a customer that looks like they need help, ask them. Some customers will never ask for help, they will just leave and try somewhere else.

This must be avoided at all costs. If possible, greet every customer as they enter the store.

Other methods may include phones throughout the store for customers to use to get assistance, a customer service booth, or any other way to make assistance readily available to the customers.

6) **Be friendly and smile.**

Nothing puts a customer at ease faster than a friendly face and a smile. Project an image that says that you are sincere in your efforts to help your customers. Always remember that your customers must have a certain level of trust in you when they ask for your assistance or recommendation. A smile and friendly face are the first steps to establishing that trust.

The Cost of Quality Customer Service

So far we have talked about making the customer feel at ease and making our business customer friendly. We talked about the value of our customers and the desire to keep them your customer and away from the competition. You may be already saying to yourself, "Hey, this is going to cost money!" Yes, it will cost money. Not as much as you think but it will cost money. The reality is, however, that it will cost you more if you **don't** do it!

Every customer a business has is considered an asset. Money has already been spent to get that customer to come into your store or call your company to place an order. Once that person does business with your company, good products and excellent service will keep them coming back time and again. The cost to keep a customer is negligible.

Now let's consider what it takes to get a new customer. In order to get a new customer, you will need advertising, promotion, marketing, and other assistance designed to motivate people to try your company. You will be competing with every other company providing the same product or service. You may incur expenses in special introductory offers or free sample offers. Whatever expenses you do incur will be charged against new business.

Industry surveys have shown that it can cost 5 - 10 times more to get a new customer than it does to keep an existing customer happy! Because of this, every effort must be made to keep your existing customers happy while trying to get new customers!

Good customer service skills allow you to gain the confidence of your customers and to correctly identify their needs. Knowing what it is your customer want enables you to effectively present options and solutions that will make the customer happy while saving your company money!

One more important reason for keeping existing customers is for referral or word of mouth business. We have already talked briefly on the importance of referral business. Where do you think referral business comes from? It comes from your customers that have done business with your company for a certain amount of time. These customers have usually purchased from your company several times and have developed a certain level of confidence in you and your company.

When this level of confidence reaches a certain point, the customer feels comfortable in referring their friends and neighbors to your business.

New customers, on the other hand, are not so quick to refer you to others. New customers feel the need to get to know your company better and assure themselves that your company is a company they can recommend to others with confidence.

A successful business grows by adding new customers to a solid base of existing customers. New customers make the business grow and also replace customers that leave.

Why do Customers Leave?

Customers will cease doing business with a company once they perceive that they are not getting the proper value for their patronage. This means that the customer will go to your competition if the customer does not feel they are getting enough service or a competitive price from you.

It is important that you understand that very often customers consider both price and service when making their decision to buy from you or not. Service and price go hand in hand when it comes to giving a customer the most value for their business. Fail to deliver what the customer expects on either of these areas and you run the risk of losing a customer.

Take a moment to think about how different businesses portray themselves. If you look at their advertising closely, you will see that the well known companies have stressed either price or service in their ads.

In some cases, you will see both areas stressed. Depending on the products or services sold, one area may be more important than the other.

Take your local warehouse clubs. These businesses stress low prices. Their appeal lies with low prices and volume purchases. Service is not a major issue. They don't accept coupons, have no sales force to assist you, and you sometimes have to put up with long lines to pay for your purchases. In these cases, the focus is on price only, not service.

Other companies will focus on the reliability of their products. Just about everyone has seen the commercials about the lonely washing machine repairman that works on one common brand of washing machine. This commercial, and the company's print advertising, stresses reliability and quality, not price. Service is the focus in these cases, not price.

The reality of the situation is that both price and service factor into just about every consumer or business decision. Failure to at least consider price and service related issues will often result in the failure of a product or business. In order to have the highest chance of success, it is crucial that both price and service issues are evaluated constantly.

You will often see both factors addressed in print and media advertising. A perfect example is automobile sales. It doesn't make any difference which dealer you buy your car from. The car will be made in the same factory, by the same workers. What will influence your decision? Both price and service!

When you buy a car from a dealer, you are not tied to that dealer for service. You can go to any dealer you want when you have a problem. Because of this, price becomes a greater part of your decision. You will go to a few dealers and see who will give you the best price. When you have a problem, you go to the dealer with the best service reputation.

Since the dealer will usually make more profit on the service of the vehicle, it is important to the dealer that you come back to his dealership when you need service. Since most people return to the dealer where they purchased the car, it is smart to focus on both price and service when promoting your business.

Whenever a business fails in it's attempts to give a customer what he or she wants, they run the risk of that customer taking their business elsewhere. Millions of dollars are spent every year getting people to buy a certain product or brand of product over the competition. Once the purchase is made, how the company responds to that customer will carry more weight than even the best advertising campaign.

The basic key to understanding why customers leave is that you must address all the customer's needs and expectations because........

Customers Have Choices & Freedom!

It's never ceases to amaze me that some people never grasp the concept that **customers have choices as to where they spend their money!** When we get our paychecks every week, we are not told where we must buy our food, clothing, or other purchases. We are left to decide where we **want** to purchase certain things. We have the right to patronize our local merchants or buy mail order. We can purchase American-made products or buy foreign products. The only restrictions we have is the amount of money we have to spend and the amount of inconvenience we will put up with.

Living in a country where this kind of freedom exists places a wealth of opportunity and choices in front of the average consumer. It also gives the consumer a tremendous amount of power over the companies that produce the goods and services they purchase. If a consumer does not feel appreciated at a specific store, they can go elsewhere! It's as simple as that!

Even when people are under a contract to do business with a certain company for a certain period of time, they are free to go to someone else after that contract expires. They may even have legal grounds to have their contracts ruled invalid.

The important thing to remember is that **every customer has the right to do business with whom they choose, for however long they choose, and that they can change their mind at any time for any reason!**

This may seem basic and sort of common sense to you but it is a very important concept that you should understand completely if you are to have a future in customer service.

The key to building and sustaining a profitable business is to give the customer what they want, when they want it, and at a price they feel is fair and that you can make a profit! It's a simple sentence that is difficult to fulfill!

Your business can only survive if you keep your existing customers happy and coming back as you try to bring new customers into your store. The only way you can do that is by addressing their needs and by giving them no reasons to look at your competition!

Now that we understand the necessity of keeping our existing customers happy, and the value they represent to us, we need to start working on........

Developing a Plan for Success!

Just like a coach prepares a game plan for the next game, you must take a look at you job or business and develop your own plan for success.

It makes no difference whether you are the owner of a multi million dollar business or a retail clerk on your first job right out of school. In order to achieve success, you need to develop your own plan for success.

What is a plan for success? Your plan for success will be like a roadmap for your business or career. It will include objectives, goals, lists of things that need to be done to achieve your goals, and a timeline for each item. You will use this plan as a guide to follow. You will change or modify it often. Your goals may change or your situation may change. Your plan will be adjusted accordingly.

How do you develop your plan? The key word is develop. You don't just sit down one day and write out your plan in five minutes on the back of a napkin.

Your plan should be thought out over days, weeks, or even months depending on you situation and goals. You will start out with a crude outline and gradually define and expand different goals and thoughts.

The first thing you will need to address is what your **primary goal** is at this moment. This goal will probably change as you progress but, for now, determine what it is you want to achieve.

Your primary goal might be to further your career. It may be to increase your customer service skills. You may wish to start your own business at a later date and want to improve your skills. Your primary goal is what you desire the end result of all your efforts.

It is important to remember that the goal you have now will change often during the process. As you achieve results, or fail to achieve results, your goals will need to be modified accordingly. For example, if you set a goal of owning your own business, once you own your own business that goal might change to increasing the size of your business at a certain rate. Your goals should always be adjusted so that you remain challenged at all times but the goals are still obtainable.

Once you have your primary goal established, you need to know what needs to happen for you to achieve that goal. What skills do you need? What education is required? What other factors will increase the likelihood of achieving your goal? What can you do to prepare yourself for making your goal a reality?

Using customer service as an example, you want to increase the customer satisfaction level of your customers by 10% in the next year. That is your goal. Now you need to figure out what you need to do to make that happen! Should you initiate new programs or procedures? Do you need customer service skills training? Do you need to do research to find out what the problems are?

Write down everything you can think of that needs to be done or will help you achieve your goal. Include anything no matter how silly or foolish it may seem. What you are doing at this point is making a list of possible actions to be taken.

Your Self-Assessment

Next, take a moment to do a **self-assessment.** A self-assessment is how you view your abilities, personality, and strengths and weaknesses. Write down what you feel are your strong points and weak points. Be brutally honest with yourself. Remember that no one will see this except yourself unless you choose to share it with someone.

The self-assessment is very important because it can help identify areas that will help you or hinder you in achieving your goals. Having this knowledge will allow you to take action on those areas that will help you achieve the goal.

For example, if your goal is increasing customer satisfaction but your self-assessment reveals that you are irritable and rude to people, that would indicate an area for action and improvement. You surely cannot increase customer satisfaction if you are rude to your customers.

The opposite would also be true. If you discover that one of your strengths is related to customers and making them feel at ease with you, that would indicate an area where immediate improvement may not be needed.

The key to your self-assessment is honesty. You are not trying to win any popularity contests or prove yourself better or worse than anyone else. Your only goal should be to accurately assess your strengths and weaknesses. Once you know your strengths and weaknesses, you can work on a plan to address those areas that need immediate improvement and make future plans to address other areas.

Knowing your strengths and weaknesses also enables you to use these to your advantage. All situations have multiple solutions or avenues of approach. If you know what you are good at and what you are not good at, you can develop a course of action that makes use of your strengths. You would avoid the solutions that require skills that you are poor in.

Areas that should be addressed in your self-assessment should include, but not be limited to, the following:

Listening Skills
Communication Skills
Appropriate appearance
Education - general
Education - specific to your job
Knowledge of product
Knowledge of company rules and procedures
Telephone skills

Conflict Resolution skills
Diversity skills (Getting along with different people)
Common sense and reasoning ability
Self confidence
Ability to work within a team

This is only a listing of a few of the areas that you should consider. The ideal way to formulate your own list would be to sit down and think of every skill you believe you would need to achieve your goal. Also include any personality trait that you believe would be an asset. Don't try to get too specific or think that anything is too minor to write down. Let the list get as long as it can. The more information you get, the better your end result will be.

When you get everything written down, try to take each item and decide whether it is a skill, personality, or educational item. Group them all together.

After you do this, you will probably find several items on each list that are basically the same. For example, if you have "problem solving" and "arriving at solutions to problems" on your list, cross one of them off. The end result will be a listing of what you feel is important for you to learn.

Now take your list and rate each item according to its importance. Make the most important item number 1 and continue until all items are done. If you have items on your list that require prior action in order to achieve, make sure you assign the prior action a higher priority. For example, if you need to finish a level two course and you have not taken level one yet, make sure that you assign taking the level one course a higher priority! Do this for all groups that you have. You should have one list for skills, one list for education, and so on.

Your assessment should reflect both good and bad traits. Good traits are those traits that lend themselves well to furthering your goals and helping you perform at a higher level. Some examples of good traits would be:

Friendly personality
Patience
Outgoing personality
Appearance
Listening Skills
Sincerity

Negative traits are those traits that prevent you from performing at your very best. They stand in the way of you achieving your goals. Some examples of negative traits would be:

Bad temper
Lack of patience
Lack of compassion
Shy

You may find that the same traits can be both good and bad depending on the situation. For example, in some cases, such as sales, being outgoing and aggressive is almost mandatory. However, if your job requires you to do other tasks besides selling, outgoing and aggressive many be a bad trait. For example, sales requires aggressive behavior. Your job is to get the customer to buy **now!** You want to close that sale before the customer leaves the store. Customer service skills involved in refunds or service, however, require patience and a low-key approach to avoid escalating the problem.

If your job consists of multiple responsibilities, you may want to treat each major responsibility on its own and develop a separate list of traits for each.

Personality traits are a very important part of our assessment. Our personalities determine how we function and interact with others. Customer Service requires a specific set of traits in order to be successful.

The basic traits for general Customer Service would include the following:

Compassion
Friendly personality
Patience
Listening skills
Self-confidence
Possesses common sense

When you are done, take the top item for each list and write it down. This will be your list of your most important objectives. These are the things you should address first and foremost. When these are addressed and resolved, move on down the list until you reach the bottom.

Making Your Assessment More Accurate!

Just like anything else, your self-assessment will only be as good as the effort you put into it. Take the time required to do the job completely. The following are some things you may want to do to make your assessment more accurate and complete:

Ask a friend or co-worker to evaluate you and your performance. Sometimes "outsiders" will see things differently than you do. They will see things that you are totally unaware of. Use their input but choose the person carefully. You must feel that this persons input will be honest and accurate and not biased by any negative feelings.

If you are unsure about certain skills or personality traits, have someone role play certain situations with you and critique your performance. This is also very valuable in practicing new skills. Use this information to validate your skill levels.

If possible, record some conversations you have with customers. (This may be illegal in some areas, consult your company for further information.) Play back the tapes and evaluate what you said and how you handled the situation. What did you do well? What did you do wrong? What made things go better? What did you do that made things worse? Use this information to determine strengths and weaknesses.

Keep a diary. When something comes up that went really wrong, make some notes about it. Try and think about what could have been done better. The same thing should be done when something goes perfectly. What did you do that made things go right? How can you apply the same techniques to other situations.

To this point, you have taken the time to make your own self-assessment. Hopefully you have asked for, and received, input from others and have also included that in your assessment. You have targeted some specific areas for improvement and have determined the most important items to tackle first. If you have done this, GREAT! You have a major advantage over the vast majority of individuals! Now is the time to take it to the next level!

Taking Action!

The best made plans for success will all fail if one important step is not taken. That step is called taking action. Taking action refers to taking whatever steps are necessary to make you plan work!

If we allow others to do things for us, we can never control where our lives will take us. If we determine we need to attend a class in order to achieve our goals, but we wait and wait until our company brings that class in-house, we may never, ever get the chance to take the course! What we need to do is to determine what exactly it is that we need NOW, and take whatever steps are necessary to get it! You need to attend a specific course, get on the phone, find out where it's given, and sign up for it!

We want to follow a specific sequence of events. That is: Identify the need, identify what must occur to achieve the desired result, and take action to achieve the result. When this is completed, we start over on the next item on our list.

Always be the one looking for ways to achieve your goals. Be aware that little gets done if you don't make the effort to make it happen.

Make it a Lasting Change!

In order to insure that the result of all your efforts is a lasting one; try to avoid some of the pitfalls that most people fall into. The following is a list of some of the things you should avoid:

Don't try to change everything overnight!

Very often, people try to tackle everything at once and make a massive change over night. This is a sure recipe for failure! The reason for this is two fold.

First, for most people, there is going to be several areas in need of improvement. If we do not break it up into small, manageable pieces, we will tend to get overwhelmed and feel the challenge is too great. When our minds start to think this way, we sort of self-sabotage our efforts. Break up goals into small chunks so that you can see results quickly and consistently. This will tend to keep your motivational level high.

The second reason, and the most important, is that in order for change to last, you must build skill upon skill to form a solid foundation from which to add skills in the future. We had you identify the most important items first so that these could be addressed and form the foundation on which you can add skills one by one in the future.

Our minds tend to resist change. Anything that takes us out of our "comfort zone" is not readily accepted in our minds. For this reason, taking it slow in the beginning, until we develop the proper mindset for change, will help us keep motivated and committed.

Break down major goals into smaller, easier to achieve, goals! A perfect example of this would be someone that wants to lose 100 pounds of weight. The person goes to the doctor and the doctor puts the person on a weight loss plan. Do you think the doctor will say "Follow this plan and you will lost the 100 pounds in eighteen months? Make an appointment in eighteen months and we will see how you did." I don't think so!

The doctor will break down the 100 pounds into 20 five-pound goals. The patient will be given dates for each goal. The small goals are much more achievable that a single huge goal. As the person loses the first 5 pounds, the feel pride and success for achieving that goal. This motivates them for achieving the next goal, and the next, and the next, and the next. Constant motivation, feeling success, and seeing results. That keeps you going.

Assign deadlines to all you goals!
Assigning dates to your action plan will help
you keep focused on what it is your need to do.
Deadlines tend to make us more aware of when
things have to be done. Dates also allow us to
list our action plans easily so that we can keep
an eye on what needs to be done this week,
month, or year.

Build your skills on a solid foundation. It
is of the utmost importance that you have a
solid foundation of basic skills on which to add
additional skills. If your basic skills are weak or
non-existent, you may find yourself building on
skills that are based on inaccurate information
or interpretation. Take the time you need to
insure that you have a solid understanding of
customer service basics before attempting to
learn advanced techniques.

Realize that you are human! There are
going to be times where you do the wrong thing
or make the wrong decision. It is important to
remember that you are only human and that
you are going to make a mistake now and then.
The key is to learn from your mistakes and not
repeat them. A strong case could be made that
those of us who make mistakes and learn from
them learn faster and retain the knowledge
longer! Our mind tends to learn things faster,
and retain the knowledge longer, when it has a
memory to associate with it. If the memory has
strong positive or negative emotions to it, we
remember even longer!

It is important that you not be afraid to venture into new areas and take a certain amount of risk. If you are afraid to make a decision, or take well-calculated risks, you will never realize your true potential and worth. The important thing to remember is: Make a well thought out judgment and learn from your experiences.

Customer Service Basics!

You Need the Customer, They Don't Need You!

Unless you, or your company, are a government office or a public utility, there are probably several companies that provide the same service or produce the same products as you do. This means that your customers can buy from you or your competition. They have the freedom of choice! They can buy their products or services from anyone they choose.

You, on the other hand, require customers because they are the ones that buy the products or services that pay your salary and enable you to have a roof over your head and food on the table. On this most basic level, you have a greater need for your customers than they have for you! Remember that!

For example, let's say you work for a supermarket or restaurant. In your town there are several other supermarkets and restaurants.

Your place is not customer friendly and does not make any effort to satisfy the customers. You believe your food alone should be enough.

Two other supermarkets and restaurants sell the same products and food but also take great steps in order to satisfy their customers and make them feel appreciated.

What do you think the result will be to each of these businesses? Over time, your customers will hear about the other businesses, try them out, and start doing business with them. Eventually, you will lose enough customers that you will have to close your doors due to lack of income.

Who suffers in these cases? The customer doesn't. He buys his products from the other market or restaurant where he felt appreciated and wanted. The only people that lose are those in your market or restaurant. **Every customer lost is a customer gained by the competition. Every dollar lost is a dollar gained by the competition.**

Your efforts should focus on customer retention. Make your customers happy and they will come back again and again. They will also recommend you to others!

Be Positive!

In sales, service, or customer service, how we talk to our co-workers, customers, and other people determines our level of effectiveness and success.

Very often two different people will offer the same solution to the same person and it will be turned done one time and accepted the next! Why is this?

Most of the time it is the way we convey our message more than the actual message. If we take time to phrase things properly, and plan out our responses, we will stand a much better chance of success. In order to learn how to phrase our message, we need to understand how the human mind responds to different words.

When we hear negative sounding words such as can't, won't, not, no, etc., our minds sometimes shut down and refuse to hear anything else the person is saying to us. The negative words mean that we are not getting what we want and we react in a negative manner. The big problem with this is that you may follow up negative comments with extremely positive ones and the other party may not even hear them!

Try to make a conscious effort to eliminate negative words from your statements. Make every statement from the positive point of view. Here are some examples:

Wrong: I **can't** do that.
Better: Let me tell you what I can do for you.

Wrong: That's **not** my area.
Better: Let me direct you to the
person that can help you.

Wrong: I **don't** know the answer to that
question.
Better: Let me find out that
information for you.

Wrong: That's **not** possible. It's **against**
company policy.
Better: I have another
suggestion. Why don't we.........

Those examples should give you an idea of
what we are talking about. Eliminating negative
words lets your customer feel that you are
trying to help them. They will remain open
minded longer than if you use negative wording
in your responses.

The last phrase is an example of one
customer service problem. Your customers do
not care at all if something is against your
company policy. Your internal policies are your
problem not theirs. It is best never to use
company policy as an excuse. One exception to
this rule would be warranty coverage. Your
warranty has specific conditions attached to it
and it is proper to use these conditions in your
conversations with the customer. In these cases,
you are using a policy to insure that all
customers are being treated equally and fairly
regarding warranty claims.

By using positive sounding statements you will decrease the time it takes to resolve issues and keep you customers open minded for a longer period of time. This is crucial to resolving issues in a win-win fashion.

You should always remember that in customer service you must keep the lines of communication open. If communication stops, or is only happening one-way, your chances for success are doomed.

Always Try To Give the Customer More Than What They Expect!

Do you want to have a customer for life? The next time you have a customer with a problem, give them more than what they expect! See how fast you can turn a negative experience into a customer for life!

Very often, a business will try to determine exactly what their customers want. Then they go ahead and design a plan to provide those needs to their customers. This method usually fails! Why? It fails because customers change their level of expectations day by day. What may satisfy a customer today may anger them tomorrow! Because of this, you must make every effort today to exceed your customers expectations! By trying to exceed expectations, you will allow yourself a little room between what you can provide and what your customers want.

For example, let's say you have windows in your home that require repair. You figure that it will take two or three weeks to get someone to your home. You call for service and get an appointment the next week. Since the company exceeded your expectations, you are happy and satisfied.

Suppose that prior to calling for service you talk to your neighbor about the windows. He tells you the last time he needed service; the man was there the next day. This will change the level of your expectations before you call the window company. If you are told that someone would be at your home next week, what do you think your reactions would be?

Your reaction would be negative because you expected service within a day or two. Since your expectations were not met, you have a negative feeling about the windows and the company that services them.

One very important thing to remember is that the level of expectations set by your customers may be reasonable or unreasonable. You may not be able to exceed someone's expectations if they are set unreasonably high. In cases such as these, we just strive to do the best we can.

The key here is to create an environment that never ceases to find ways to increase customer satisfaction and provide extra value to the customer.

It is important to realize that while you are trying to improve your customer service, your competitors are doing the same. Your continuing efforts are your only defense in insuring that your business stays on top month after month, year after year.

Balancing the Customers Needs vs. Company Needs

We have just talked about giving the customer more than what they expect. In order to do this, and remain a profitable company, we must always know what costs are associated with satisfying a customer. Once we know the costs involved, we can make a determination whether or not we wish to approve a certain course of action.

We have already talked about the value of a customer. We stated that the value of a customer is not the value of his or her last purchase. Rather, the real value of a customer is the amount of products or services they purchase, how often they purchase them, how long you anticipate they will continue to purchase, and the amount of word of mouth advertising the customer may represent.

When we know the value of a customer, we also get an idea concerning what we may want to spend to make that customer happy.

If a customer spends thousands of dollars a year with your company, you may find it acceptable to spend one or two hundred dollars on a solution to satisfy that customer. If that same customer spent fifty dollars with your company over the last five years, you would not consider spending one hundred dollars to make him happy.

(There may be certain situations where you may feel it worthwhile, but generally you would not spend that amount of money in this situation.)

Businesses are in business for one reason, to make money. They make money by selling products or services to their customers at a price that is higher than what it costs to product the product or service. The difference between the cost of producing the product or service and the selling price is called **profit.** There are basically two types of profit. Gross profit and net profit.

Gross profit is the difference between the cost of making the product or service and it's selling price. For example, if it costs your company $10 to make a widget, and you charge $25 for it, the gross profit would be $15. Gross profits do not include items such as overhead (rent, utilities, office salaries, equipment, etc.) or the cost of supporting and marketing the product.

Net profit is the amount of profit that the company makes after all costs involved in making, marketing, supporting, and selling the product have been deducted.

This is the amount of money that the company has actually made by selling the product.

For example:

A widget sells for $25. It costs $10 to produce, $1 to market, $2 to support, and $3 to sell, including overhead.

The net profit would be $25 less $16 in costs. The net profit would be $9.

Why should we be concerned with net profits in Customer Service? Because everything we do, everything we offer a customer, every action we take, every solution we arrive at, has a cost associated with it. The more expensive our actions are, the more it costs the company. These charges are added to other costs and are subtracted from the gross profits. If support and warranty costs are too high, serious repercussions can take place.

Let's take the same widget. It sells for $25. It costs $10 to make and another $6 in support and other expenses. The unit is guaranteed for one year. Due to a manufacturing problem, one part of the unit fails in six months. Since most every unit will fail within the warranty period, a replacement will have to be sent to everyone who purchased one. The cost of this; $10 to produce the new unit, $2 to ship and package each unit, and $1 in other expenses. In short, it costs the company $13 to supply the new unit to the customer. If you remember that our original net profit was $9, you now can see that the company will lose $4 on each unit sold. ($9 - $13 for replacement = $4 loss)

Sometimes these situations have only one solution. In most cases, however, there are multiple solutions. You should always try and search for the most cost-effective solution to a specific situation. In the above example, it might have been possible to ship a replacement part to the owner with instructions on how to install it.

This saves the customer the inconvenience of returning the unit and you will save on costs. This is a win-win situation!

In this case, the cost of the part may be $2 plus $1 for shipping. Add $1 for other expenses and your total becomes $4. Subtract that from our $9 gross profit and you still have a $5 profit left on every item sold. Not as good as $9 but a lot better than a $4 loss!

Very often a company's success or failure lies with the decisions that are made on a daily basis. Only when the costs of those decisions are understood can a good, sound decision be made. Always consider the costs of every solution before presenting them to the customer. If possible, present the least costly options first and save the very expensive ones for last ditch attempts to satisfy the customer.

Learning From Past Experiences

Do you want to know why some people succeed and other fail? Successful people realize the value of learning from their mistakes and refusing to make the same mistakes over and over again. They take a situation, analyze it, and determine what has to be done to insure that the problem doesn't come up again. Then they move on to the next problem.

The same can be said for businesses. A successful business adapts to different situations. When a problem arises, they investigate the problem to make sure that a problem does, in fact, exist. Very often someone will perceive that a problem exists only to find out later that the information was false.

If a problem does exist, different solutions are examined until the best solution is found. That solution is then implemented in order to eliminate that specific problem from occurring in the future.

A good example of this is the example we used in a previous discussion. Suppose the widget with the defective part just kept being made with that same part year after year. No one took time to determine what the problem was; they just replaced the unit when it broke. The widget was just one product the company produced. Other products were profitable and the company made money so who cares? This is a recipe for failure! When ever a problem presents itself:

Investigate it to make sure it exists.
Determine the cause of the problem.
Arrive at multiple solutions.
Pick best solution
Implement solution.

Most successful people and businesses follow this approach when problems arise. There is one more step, however, that separates the "men from the boys" in their level of success. That step is called **Follow Up.**

When we investigate a problem and arrive at a solution, there is rarely a situation where we are 100% certain that we have uncovered the whole problem and that we have chosen the proper and best solution. The only way we can be absolutely certain is by continually monitoring the situation after we have introduced changes. Does the problem go away? Has everything gone as expected? Have things occurred as fast as we thought? What new problems or concerns have surfaced?

All these questions, and more, must be answered over time before we can close the issue and move on. Making changes and not monitoring the results creates an environment with a dangerous future.

Changing the Way You Look at Complaints!

If you were to ask the vast majority of people involved in Customer Service how they feel about complaints, the average reaction would be extremely negative. That's a normal and expected reaction. There is another way, however, to look at complaints.

Complaints should be viewed as opportunities. When someone complains, they are letting you know that something is not right with your product or service. In most cases, their complaints are actually opportunities for you to make things right and keep that customer coming back!

Suppose you went to the doctor and the doctor told you that there was a disease spreading around that had no symptoms whatsoever until death. How would you react to that? Not very positively I would imagine! The same would apply to a company with problems that received no complaints.

When you get sick, your body gives you indications that something is going wrong. You may start with a sore throat and get worse. The sore throat and worsening symptoms let you know you should seek medical attention. The symptoms warn you before it's too late. No symptoms, no treatment, you die!

In business, your customer complaints allow you to discover product or service problems that exist within your company. By making you aware of problems, you then have the opportunity to make changes to eliminate the problems. What would happen if you received no complaints? You could possibly continue to product a problem product and lose customer to your competition without ever knowing why! Then, all of a sudden, one day you realize you have no customers and, even worse, you have no idea why! That is a business "death"!

The other opportunity that you are given when someone has a complaint is the opportunity to show that customer just how good you and your company is! You can turn a negative situation around and gain a customer for life if you take the right approach!

Most people are rational and reasonable when they first experience a problem. It's only when things happen to make the problem worse that these same people get rude and unreasonable. Make every effort to understand what the customer is experiencing and take whatever steps required to address their problems. You could possibly gain a customer for life!

The absolute worst thing you can do to a customer is to make them feel that they are an inconvenience or a nuisance. Just about every business makes their customers feel appreciated when they make a purchase. It's how those same customers are treated when problems arise that is a good Customer Service indicator of that company!

The Importance of Appearance!

The issue of appearance is a very important and very sensitive issue. The appearance on an individual is subject to interpretation by the customer and those that work with the individual. Very often, the first impression of a person is based on the appearance of that person.

Stated in its most basic form, the appearance of an individual in the business environment should be appropriate for the industry in which that person is employed.

For example, if you were to go to an investment banker to invest your life savings, you would not feel comfortable if the person you met came out in cut off shorts and an old T-shirt. The accepted level of dress in that situation would be a suit and tie. Preferably a dark suit and conservative tie.

If you were to hire someone to clean your pool, or trim your bushes, you would not expect a suit and tie but rather shorts and an old T-shirt. This would be the expected and appropriate appearance for that job.

Unless you have good reasons to differ from what is considered appropriate dress and appearance, it is smart to provide the customer with the appearance and image they expect. Since we should be striving to inspire confidence and security in the minds of our customers, we should concentrate on how we as employees represent our company.

Appearance covers several different areas. It consists of dress, personal hygiene and grooming, as well as the type of physical body we have. Some, or all of these, may be a factor in your success in serving your customers.

Like it or not, our appearance is what we are first judged on when we meet a customer for the first time. Our appearance may determine whether or not the customer will even listen to us. Appearance may also be the determining factor as to whether the customer will talk with you or seek out another individual!

We all have pre-conceived ideas about how certain professions should look and act. Doctors, for example, should be middle-aged, friendly people in white coats with a nice smile. They should be well groomed and neat. Anything that differs from this perception will raise a bit of suspicion in our minds.

Another very frustrating thing is that our appearance may cause people to make judgements on our technical or job abilities based on appearance! This can be a tough hurdle to jump! Let's take a look at an example:

You get a phone call from a hospital that a family member has been in a bad accident. You get to the hospital and a doctor comes out to talk to you. He is middle aged, dressed in a white coat and collar and tie. Hair is short and well groomed. He gives you details and asks you to consent to a specific course of treatment. He leaves and a few minutes later another doctor comes out, introduces himself, and tells you he is also familiar with the case. He is fairly young looking, wearing jeans and a flowered shirt. His hair is quite long and not very well groomed. He has a two-day growth of beard. He recommends a completely different course of action and asks for your consent. Which course of action will you agree to?

Chances are you will tend to agree with the first doctor unless you have been given information from other sources. Why? Because the first doctor has an appearance that you feel comfortable with. It inspires confidence. Since it inspires confidence and makes you feel comfortable, your mind automatically generates an opinion that this person also has superior skills. An opinion based on fact? No! An opinion based on appearance. The opinion may be right or wrong but it is still based on the wrong kind of information.

In the case of the doctors, the first doctor may be a borderline physician that has handled only a few cases like yours in his whole career! You don't know that. The second doctor could be a specialist in cases like yours with the highest success rate in his profession! You will exclude him based on appearance alone unless you receive input from someone else. It may not be fair but it is human nature!

In Customer Service every effort should be made to present an appearance that is not offensive to the customer. Personal hygiene is very important. No one likes to be near anyone that is dirty or has an odor about him or her. Your appearance should inspire confidence in you and your company. Your appearance should give the impression of confidence and competence. Your appearance should also give the impression of someone that is organized and knowledgeable. Once you realize the importance of your appearance, the easier it is to change for the better.

If there is any doubt as to how you should look in your job, take a look at the other people that work with you and for your competition. How do they dress? What do they do that you don't do? Is there something that everyone does that you don't? How can you change your appearance to make you more effective? These are the questions that you should ask yourself.

Legal issues may also come into play here. While it may be advantageous to hire a specific kind of person to fit a certain job, there are laws about discriminating against people on the basis of age, sex, and other factors.

If in doubt, consult with your attorney before hiring.

Another way of looking at this is to examine the way we advertise in our county. Every aspect of a commercial is planned out well in advance. The way people look, how they are dressed, the scenery behind them, everything down to the minutest detail is studied and analyzed before the commercial is put on the air or placed in print. The entire reason for this is that the company wants to create an image that addresses all our pre-conceived notions about the product or service they are selling. If these major corporations spend this must attention on appearances, how important do you think you appearance is to your job and your company?

Compassion, Concern & Sincerity

The Big Three of Customer Service

Do you know what your customers really want from you and your business? They want to be cared for and cared about. They want to feel appreciated and needed? Is that really so much to ask? After all, you are asking these same people to give you their hard-earned money in exchange for your product or service. That's a pretty big request!

When you are dealing with a customer it is important that you show concern for their needs and desires. By spending the time to ask the right questions, you are showing your customer that you have a sincere desire to help them make the correct purchase the first time. Think about the kind of impression that you would make if a customer asked you a question about a product and you replied, "Oh, try this one.

We sell more of this than anything else. It probably will do the trick." The impression of the customer would be that you could care less what the customer bought.

If that same customer asked the same question and you proceeded to ask him questions about his needs until you identified the correct product, do you think the customer would have a different opinion of you? Of course. The customer would realize that you took the time to help them and they would have a certain degree of faith in you. These feeling would also carry over to the customer's perception of your company. How you represent yourself to the customer is how you represent your company to the customer.

Compassion also plays an important part in Customer Service. When people come to other people with a problem, they want the other person to care about their problem and to attempt to understand it. They do not want to get the feeling that their problems are of little concern to others. This is where the compassion comes into play.

When someone comes to you with a problem, take the time to understand it and communicate your sincere desire to help resolve the problem. Let your customer know that you understand their feelings and that you intend to do anything you can to resolve it. Do not brush the customer off. Always keep in mind that we need the customer more than they need us! Don't be afraid to show compassion to your customers.

That does not mean you have to admit responsibility when the customer is at fault. What it does mean is that you should take the time to listen to your customer's problems and make an effort to understand them. This is what we mean about compassion.

When we talk about concern, we are talking about your ability to be genuinely concerned about your customers. Being concerned means purchasing the right products for certain applications, giving them service when they need it, and always being aware of their needs. We have even heard of a salesman that calls a few of his customers the week before an item goes on sale. He knows they purchase the item on a regular basis so he makes sure they are aware of the sale! What does this say to the customer? They are blown away by the fact that the salesman remembered them and what they purchased. They become aware that their business is appreciated! And the salesman gets more sales in the process!

It should be noted that most people can spot a phony a mile away. If you are not sincere in your thoughts and actions it will be very obvious to most people. Sincerity is not something that can be practiced and mastered. Sincerity can only come by learning to appreciate your customers and what they represent to you. As you begin to respect your customers you will start to want to help them. As you go through this process, your honest sincerity will start to grow by itself.

Three Important Keys to Quality Customer Service!

Listen, Listen, and Listen!

When you go to a doctor, does the doctor come in, look at you, and tell you where you're hurting? Of course not! Your doctor will ask you questions and, based on your answers, make a diagnosis. The same thing is done in Customer Service.

In order to be effective in Customer Service, you need to develop great listening skills. Listening skills enable you to accurately determine what must be done in a certain situation to resolve a problem. Without proper information, the rest of the process is doomed to fail miserably.

When we refer to listening skills, we are talking about much more than listening to the customer talk.

Good listening skills applies to listening to what the other person is saying and picking out the important and relevant information and discarding information that is emotional in nature rather than factual. For example, if a customer is dissatisfied about the quality of a product, he or she will also tend to complain about the salesman, the delivery person, and anyone else that was involved with the purchase. Were these other people part of the problem? They might be but the primary problem remains the quality issue.

If there were one key rule to listening it would be **do not interrupt the other person while they are talking.** Letting a person talk accomplishes two very important things. First, it lets the person vent their frustrations and feelings. This venting tends to reduce feelings of anger and allows you a greater chance of resolving the issue. Second, letting the person talk gives you an opportunity to pick up little bits of information that may never come out during standard questioning. Just one bit of information may give you a clue as to the real problem that exists.

When listening to someone describing a problem to you, make yourself aware to words or phrases that come up several times. If the other person continually makes reference to a specific item or condition, this is a clear indicator that this item or condition carries a lot of weight with the person.

For example, elderly people, or people on a fixed income, tend to be more sensitive about costs involved in the problem. If the customer says "I paid a lot for this product and I don't want it repaired. I want it replaced! What will happen after the warranty period is up? This unit is defective and I want a new unit so I won't have to purchase another one two years from now!"

If you look at what the customer said, you will notice that there were three separate statements made regarding price. The first one was that they paid a lot for the product. That one was easy. Next comes the comment about the end of the warranty. The customer is referring to the cost of future repairs after the warranty. Again, a money issue. The last reference to money is the statement about not wanting to have to purchase again in two years. This refers to both money and long term confidence in the product.

By understanding exactly the areas of greatest concern to the other party, we can design solutions to the problem that are aimed towards these same areas of concern. In the example above, a successful solution would be keyed to money and restoring the confidence in the product. If your company produced the product, an offer to extend the warranty period may be all that is required. If that is not an option, perhaps a discount towards a future purchase may make the person feel better. Either way, the solution must address the problem.

Another person may not place a strong emphasis on money but on time. They need the problem addressed and resolved immediately. They will pay for overnight shipping. They need things done know! How would you address that person? Would you be better off offering a discount or a solution that may cost a little more but will resolve the issue quickly and effectively? That's easy! You would opt for the solution that resolves the problem quickly! Why? Because that is what the customer has indicated is the most important aspect of the problem.

Why should we try to identify the primary areas of concern? The first reason is obvious. If we identify what the real problem is and address those issues, we will have a far greater chance of resolving the problem quickly and make the customer happy.

The second reason is that solutions that address the primary areas of concern are far more likely to be more cost effective. Think about it. If someone offers you something that addresses all your concerns, won't you tend to be happy with the solution and agree to it? If the solution solves the problem but doesn't address your particular areas of concern, don't you think that you would try to get more from the other party to compensate? Most people will try to get just that. Address the areas of concern with your solutions and make every effort to identify and address every known issue.

Taking the time to listen to what your customers are saying also lets your customers feel that you are concerned about their problems and do not wish to just pass those problems to someone else. It also lets them know that you have a sincere desire to help them. (There are those words again! Sincere. Concerned.) It is important to remember that when a customer has a problem they are in a situation where they are at your mercy. They depend on you to assist them in resolving their problems. If they sense that you do not care about their situation, they will assume a defensive position. When a customer gets in a defensive position, the cost of resolving the problem increases.

Listening to your customer's helps to resolve problems more quickly, more cost effectively, and helps you build customer satisfaction and loyalty! Listen to what we're saying. It works!

The Golden Rule!

If you remember back to when you first started school, you were probably taught this "Golden Rule": "Do onto others as you would have them do onto you." Simply put, this means to treat others like you would want to be treated. There is no one place where this is more true than in Customer Service.

The basis for any business relationship is a mutual trust between two parties. The customer must trust the business and the business must trust the customer. If one part of this arrangement does not exist the entire relationship will ultimately fail.

We do a lot in business to make our business customer friendly and easy to do business with. Part of our motivation is money made by keeping your customers coming back time and time again. The other part of our motivation comes from **respect for our customer and our business.** A good business knows the value of respect for the customer. As previously discussed, respect means sincerity.

When we deal with our customers, it is important that we treat them like we would want to be treated if we were in their situation. This means making the effort to go the extra mile and take steps to make the interaction as pleasant as possible.

When you put your customer at ease, it becomes much easier to deal with problems or other negative solutions. Putting the customer at ease means be friendly, showing compassion, and making a sincere effort to resolve the issue at hand.

One of the most effective methods of dealing with people is to ask yourself how you would feel if you were be told the same thing that you are going to tell your customer. If you ask yourself how you would feel, you will accomplish two things.

First, you can get a good indication if your response is worded correctly and presented properly. If you have any negative feelings about what you are thinking about saying or doing, try and figure out how to present your thoughts more effectively.

Second, if you have objections to a particular course of action or wording, you will give yourself the opportunity to respond to those feelings or at least develop a response for them if the customer should have the same response. You will have a much more effective response if you have a chance to think about it beforehand.

It is also more important to remember that there should not be any losers in any customer service situation. In order to make the customer happy and the business profitable; we should always strive for a resolution where both parties win. This is called a win-win situation. Win-win situations do not create hard feelings for any party involved. Everyone wins in a good resolution.

Take a moment and think about what happens when you resolve an issue with a solution that blatantly favors the company or the customer. If you give away the store to make someone happy, your company will lose money and possibly fail. If you resolve an issue and the customer feels they were taken advantage of, they will not come back and everyone loses.

If you approach every issue with the sincere desire to be fair to all parties, you will tend to arrive at solutions that will be acceptable to all involved. Never try to put one over on a customer. They may be happy today but angry tomorrow when they realize that they have been taken advantage of.

Keeping Customers in the Right Frame of Mind

We have talked a lot about being responsive to the needs of our customers. The reason for this is that we need to keep our customers in the right frame of mind so that we can interact with them in a productive manner.

That may sound like quite a mouthful but what it means is this: If we can continue to make our customers feel at ease with us, they will listen to what we have to say. Think about that for a moment.

If we allow our customers to get angry and upset with us or our company, they are going to come into any discussion with a negative attitude and will not tend to want to listen to anything we have to say. When this occurs, we have to spend time and money just to get the person to the point that they agree to listen to us. This wasted time and money benefits no one.

If you deal in an industry where your work is done via appointment, you must remember that keeping someone waiting for extended periods of time often results in trouble.

While most people understand about delays and emergency situations, they still expect to be served in an appropriate time frame. If they experience continual delays and wait times, they will find another place to take their business. More on that later.

Frame of mind is also the result of how the customer has been treated prior to this visit. If they had a pleasant experience before, they will be more tolerant of you when a problem arises. If their previous experience was bad, they will have little tolerance for you and your company and may even go out of their way to create problems.

An interesting study revealed that it could take up to ten good experiences to wipe out the effects of a single bad experience. This means that if your customer came into your store and had a bad experience, it could take ten more trips to your business to convince them that the bad experience was not a normal occurrence. Because of this, we must make a sincere effort to minimize the chances for a bad experience. The next few topics will deal with minimizing the chances of a bad experience.

Serving Customers on Time

Do you think it is possible to show respect to your customers if you keep them waiting and waiting before you serve them. No! Unless you are the only source for a particular product or service, your customers will go to your competition if they will serve them quickly and on-time.

Making efforts to get your customers served quickly show that you respect their time and other responsibilities. We discussed wait time very briefly in the beginning of this publication. We discussed that the shorter the period of time a customer has to wait, the happier they are. Given a choice, a customer will shop at the store where they can complete the purchase as quickly as possible if price and location are equal.

In today's society, more and more homes are two-wage earner households. This means that both husband and wife work. When this is the situation, spare time for shopping and other tasks is precious.

If shopping at your business means spending a long amount of time, they will probably choose to shop elsewhere. In these cases, you are not responding to the needs of this particular group of consumers.

Another aspect of serving customers on time is in the area of delivery or service appointments. Think about how you feel when you must stay at home and wait for the deliveryman or repairman. How do you feel when they can't narrow down the time they will be at your house and make you stay home for the entire day? Not very positive, I'm sure.

If your business requires home visits and appointments, try and provide your customers with as short a time frame as possible for their service or delivery. For example, letting the customer know if it will be morning or afternoon is better than giving them just a day. Letting them know within a two-hour window would be even better! This way your customers can plan tasks for the time before the service is scheduled. They don't have to tie up their whole day and you get a good start on some great customer satisfaction! What this all boils down to is showing respect for your customers and their other responsibilities.

Speaking of appointments, how about businesses that do all their business by appointment? Doctors, dentists, and other medical personnel are prime examples of this situation. What can they do to serve their patients better?

How many times have you arrived for a 1 o'clock appointment at the doctor and find that they are 2 hours behind schedule? To make matters worse, you look at the appointment book and find that they have booked three people in that same time slot and there is only one doctor? It's amusing to find that the vast majority of people kind of expect this treatment from the medical profession but not from an interior decorator or other professional!

Times are changing; however, people are becoming more and more intolerant of having to wait for any kind of appointment, including medical. The reason is clear. People are more aware of their choices than ever before. Keep them waiting, they go to someone else down the street.

Keep in mind that when you book multiple appointments or keep someone waiting long periods of time, you are in fact saying, "Our time is more valuable than yours." That's a bad message to send a customer. You customer just might say, "I'm taking my business and money somewhere else. I'll let my friends know about this too." That's an even worse message for a business to hear!

Be Considerate of Customer Needs

The most important things bear repeating. Being considerate of the needs of your customers may be just plain common sense, but you will be surprised at the number of people and businesses that just don't care!

We have talked about respecting your customers. You cannot respect your customers and ignore their needs at the same time. It just can't be done!

Always being on the lookout for customer's needs allows you grow both as a business and as people. We talked about information and the importance of understanding just what it is that is causing a problem. We have talked about the need to address problems and eliminate future occurrences. What we need to talk about now is the needs of customers and their importance to you as an employee or business owner.

In customer service, customer needs should be viewed as opportunities. A need has a solution. Provide a product or service that meets that need and you make a sale! Make enough sales and your business grows. It really is that simple. There is no magic here, just common sense. (Those two words just keep showing up, don't they!)?

As you deal with your customers, you will get an idea about who they are and what they want. Some customers will call, or come in, and ask if you have a specific item or service for sale. In cases like these, it is easy to find out what you customer is looking for. Write down these requests and submit them to management. If enough people communicate the need for a product or service, just maybe your company should produce it! If only one person out of ten thousand ask for something, that request will usually die a quick death. But if 50 out of a hundred ask for the same thing, you better start producing it right now before someone else does!

You also will have a group of customers that will come in, walk around, and leave. They were looking for something and either didn't like what they saw or could not find it. Unless you approach these customers and ask, you will never know!

I am a strong believer in approaching every customer that even slightly looks like they need assistance.

Offering your help in a non-aggressive manner, gives you the opportunity to not only help the customer but to find out what their needs are. Think about asking every customer that is leaving your store if there was something they need but you don't carry. Again, keep track of the responses and determine the suitability of each request.

The last thing I'm going to say here about customer needs is that it is important to address as many of their needs as possible. Otherwise, you may lose a customer. Let's say that a customer needs to purchase 10 related items. You offer 5 of the items and your competition offers 9. Where do you think that customer will go? They will go where their needs are being addressed more completely.

Why do you think warehouse clubs are so popular? Because they address a wide range of needs. One stop for clothes, electronics, film, food, furniture, medicine, etc! To top it off, the prices are good also! If you don't believe this, think about this one little fact: People want to shop at warehouse clubs so much that they even pay yearly "dues" for the privilege! How many of your customers would pay dues to your company for the opportunity to buy your products?

This brings up one different aspect of meeting customer's needs. Companies that respond the best to their customers needs can often charge higher prices that their competition and still retain their customers!

The simple reason for that is that the customer feels that the combination of service and product offerings are so superior and convenient, that they are willing to pay slightly higher prices to shop at that particular business.

Showing Customers that you Care

Time for a quick review here. This is important. In order for you to achieve a satisfactory customer service level, your customers have to be convinced that you care about them. Not your company, but you! As a front line customer service person, you represent your company and the way your company feels about their customers. Give them the right impression and they will come back again and again. Give them a bad experience and you may never get the opportunity to make it up to them.

Generally speaking, the more expensive your products and services are, the more confident your customer will need to feel before they make their purchase. If they feel that you do not care about their purchase, they will go elsewhere.

Showing a customer that you care gives them the feeling that if they purchase from you that they will have someone to turn to when and if things should go wrong.

This is one area where the small businesses can have the advantage over the mega-stores and warehouse clubs! If your product or service lends itself to after sales support and service, small businesses may be able to offer more personal support than the stores that rely on high volume sales. It's surprising how many small businesses let these opportunities slip past them.

The Importance of a Quality Product or Service

We have talked about the importance of customer service in attracting new customers and retaining existing ones. The importance of that cannot be overstated. There is, however, one very important fact that must not be overlooked. **No amount of customer service training or expertise can make up for a poor quality product or service.**

It would surprise you to hear how many companies knowing produce inferior quality products. They preach about customer satisfaction and warranties but still produce inferior products. In these cases, good customer service skills may delay customer loss, but customers will leave if they are constantly presented with poor quality products or services.

Good customer service skills will only be an asset to you and your company if they are used to support and sell quality products.

Investing in customer service skills to support inferior products or services is a waste of money.

The only exception to this is when a company produces a product that is supposed to be high quality but has problems that are discovered only after the product has been released. In these cases, good customer service skills allow the company to identify the problem, keep the customer happy, and take measures to insure that the problem gets resolved in the best way possible.

Every company produces a product that fails for one reason or another once it hits the marketplace. It is how the company reacts to this situation that separates the good companies from the bad.

As a representative for your company, what should you do if you uncover a problem with one or more of your products?

We have already discussed the proper action to be taken. If you should uncover a problem with a product, take steps required to satisfy the customer you are dealing with at that time. This may call for a repair, refund, exchange, or other appropriate action. After the customer has been taken care of it is time to document the problem and inform the people in charge of that product. The information you provide will help them determine which course of action to take. Again, only with the correct amount of information can an accurate decision be made.

Problems that are left uncorrected can lead to excessive costs incurred by the company and result in the loss of customers. Your job as a front line customer service person is to insure that you get the proper information regarding the problem and forward that information to the appropriate person. Your desired result should be to get the issue resolved quickly so that it effects the minimum amount of customers.

Asking Customers Questions

Most of us are given several "tools" to use in doing our jobs. These tools may be reference materials, training, manuals, audio or videotapes, and other types of materials or aides to help you serve the customer. In order to use these materials effectively, we need to learn how to ask questions.

Why do we have to learn how to ask questions? Well, unless your company has provided you with a crystal ball, you will have no idea what your customer wants or needs unless they tell you. In most cases, you will have to ask pertinent questions in order to establish the exact information you will need.

Asking questions follows a certain type of pattern. You probably already use this pattern without even thinking about it. It is a kind of **diagnosis by elimination pattern**.

Simply put, diagnosis by elimination means that you ask question to eliminate not needed information until to find the correct result.

We accomplish this by asking a series of questions. The first question is a very broad-based question designed to narrow down the information to a general area. This eliminates many other areas of concern. Your first question might be a simple, "How can I help you today?" question. Your customer will usually tell you the type of product he is looking for. That becomes the general area.

You then ask a more specific question such as, "How big is the room you want to heat with your new heater?" This question gives you an idea of how large the heater has to be. This will eliminate many low power models and narrow down your choices. Continue with an even more specific question such as, "Do you want an automatic thermostat?" These questions will let you know what kind of options the customer wants. You continue asking questions until you narrow down the possibilities to one or two choices. These choices will have the features and correct application for the customer. The customer can then make an informed decision.

What might happen if you didn't take the time to ask questions? By not asking questions, you run the risk of selling the customer something that may not work correctly in the application the customer has in mind. The result is a customer that is not happy with their purchase and your business.

Some people take the approach that if you sell the best model to every customer you will always have a satisfied customer.

While there may be some logic in that statement, you must also consider that every customer does not need the best model and you may lose sales by always recommending the most expensive model. The correct approach is to identify exactly what the customer needs and then sell them something that will meet those needs. There is no harm in pointing out the features of the better models, some customers may want them, but always make the customer aware of every product that will fulfill their needs.

Always start off with general questions and gradually become more specific until the need is established. The more questions you ask, the greater the probability of making a correct judgement. We have discussed the importance of establishing just what the real issues are when a customer has a problem. Asking questions is the only way of correctly ascertaining the underlying problems that may exist.

Giving Customers Options

During the course of an average week, you will probably run into one or two problem situations that will have only one solution. Even a simple defective return will have options. Do you replace it, repair it, and refund the customers money?

Or upgrade the customer to a better unit? All these options have costs associated with them so you need to make decisions. How do you decide what to tell your customers?

Try and think how you react when someone gives you only one option in a given situation. How does that make you feel? Does it make you feel part of the process or does it make you feel like an outsider looking in? If you're like most people, it will tend to create a negative image if you are given no input to the solution.

For this reason, it is advisable to give the customer the option of more than one solution. Giving the customer options makes them part of the resolution process and will tend to create a more positive environment for resolving the issue in a win-win fashion.

Remember that the more positive feelings the customer has, the more cost effective it is going to be to resolve the problem or make the sale.

On the sales side, it is commonplace for a salesperson to offer several different models and brands to a customer making a purchase. The features and cost of each are given to the customer and the customer is left to making an informed decision. Most consumer and business purchases are made in this manner. This method is effective because it makes the person part of the decision making process. Once someone takes an active part in the decision making, they are much more likely to support the decision after the sale.

On the customer service side, making the customer part of the resolution process is critical to obtaining a win-win solution. If you have multiple resolutions available to you, and they have the same approximate costs associated with them, let the customer decide which course of action to take. If some of the resolutions are more costly than others, hold them back and present them only if the first set of resolutions fail to satisfy the customer.

You present your resolutions to the customer in this manner: "Mrs. Smith, I'm sorry for the problems you've been having with our product. I can replace the product with a new unit, credit the cost towards a different make or model, or refund your money. Which would you prefer?"

What have you accomplished with that statement? First you expressed concern and compassion, your have made the customer part of the process, and you have shown a sincere desire to help the customer by offering several resolutions to the problem. By offering multiple resolutions to the customer, you are also addressing the customer individual needs and preferences.

Let's compare that strategy with offering one solution. By offering one solution to the customer you are telling your customer, "Here it is. Take it or leave it!" You are not addressing the customers needs and are not letting them become part of the process. This is not a very effective strategy for resolving problems and making sales.

Always offer multiple resolutions to the customer and make them part of the resolution process. It reduces resolution time and costs. It also increases customer satisfaction.

Don't Back People into a Corner!

Whoever said the customer is always right did not work in customer service. Very often the customer is wrong, plain and simple. They bought the wrong product, assembled or installed it wrong, or did something to prevent the product from functioning properly. In some cases the product may be fine but the customer insists that it should do something that it just wasn't intended to do in the first place! How do you deal with customer like that? We all have them. They are a small percentage of our customers but they make all our jobs much harder.

The truth of the matter is that we always must remember that the customer may not always be right but the customer is still the customer. Remember that we need our customers but our customers do not necessarily need us. That in mind, there is one effective method for dealing with unreasonable people and customer caused problems. That method is called **non-confrontation.**

Non-confrontation means resolving the issue without directly assessing blame. In English, that means, give the customer an out! Never directly confront a customer and accuse them of being the cause of the problem. If you do accuse the customer, you will probably lose whatever chance you did have of resolving the issue and salvaging the relationship.

Instead, communicate to the customer in a non-confrontational manner. Make it easy for the customer to react to your comments. For example, if someone assembled something wrong, do not say, "Of course this doesn't work! You assembled this wrong! Take it home and do it right and it will work just fine!" This type of comment not only offends the customer but also is condescending in nature. You would be better off by saying; "I see the problem. This part was assembled incorrectly. I have seen this done many times. Just switch these parts around and it will work great!"

That comment lets the customer know the cause of the problem but also gives the customer an "out" by saying that others have done the same thing. It dissolves the anger generated by telling the customer they were at fault. You also have told him the parts to change and have assured the customer that the product will function just fine after the corrections have been made. If the corrections are simple, you may want to do them yourself and make the customer even more pleased with your store. Every little thing leads to customers coming back again and again!

Why do you think that being non-confrontational is important? The human mind does not react well to blame or confrontation. Once we are personally confronted or blamed for something, we tend to react in a very defensive manner. We will tend to tune out whatever is being said and will focus on only one solution. We also tend to get unreasonable and not very co-operative. This is not a recipe for making sales or solving problems. Giving the customer an "out" allows us to open meaningful two way dialogue and resolve the issues at hand quickly and more economically.

Separating Perception from Reality

If you feel you are doing a good job, but your customers perceive that you are doing a poor job, whose opinion matters? In reality, both opinions carry a great deal of weight.

It is important that you feel that you are doing a good job. You must learn from your mistakes and do the best job you are capable of. You must do the kind of job your boss thinks you should. You must also represent the company as your company wishes to be represented. If you accomplish that, you will make the management of your company happy with your performance. That's great but sometimes that is not good enough.

Our customer's expectations change over time. What was good enough 10 years ago is not acceptable today. Because of this, we must continually deal with our customer's perceptions of us and our company.

A great deal of customer service skills are based on perception. The customer must perceive that you really care about them and their needs. They must feel confident that you care about them. In reality, you may deal with a thousand customers every week. You can't possible have personal relationships with each customer when you deal with a high volume. Your customer service skills and techniques allow you to create a perception in the mind of the customer that creates that feeling of trust and caring.

You alter a person's perception of you by doing things for that customer. Perceptions can change over night or over years. Every positive experience your customer has with you and your company will make their perception of you more positive. A negative experience will have an opposite effect. As previously stated, negative impressions carry more emotional weight than positive experiences.

In order to address issues of perception it is important that we understand just what perception is and how it is formed.

A perception is nothing more than an opinion on how things are interpreted in someone's mind. They do not have to be based on reality. Perceptions are usually a mixture of how things really are and how the customer feels they should be. Two people will often perceive totally different things after evaluating a specific situation. Why is that? Different perceptions are usually due to a person having different prior feelings.

Let's say you require service for a product you purchased. In the past, you have received service within two days of requesting it. The service you get today takes 5 days. Your perception will be that the response time is very poor.

Take the same scenario, but substitute someone that had service in the past within 21 days. Their perception will be that response time was excellent! Same situation, same response time, totally different perceptions!

Perceptions are formed in someone's head from all the experiences they have had as well as friends, co-workers, neighbors, and anyone else they come in contact with. Since every experience alters one's perception you have to deal with not only the future but also everything that has happened in the past.

Perceptions can work for you or against you. If you are fortunate to work for a company with an excellent reputation, perception will work in your favor most of the time. Since an excellent reputation creates a positive perception, you will be given the benefit of the doubt based on your reputation.

Perceptions can also work against you. If your company has a poor reputation for service and inferior products, it is going to take a very long time to alter that perception. Some companies never recover from a single negative association. Other companies must fight for years to overcome a bad perception by their prospective customers.

Positive perceptions can also hurt you. If you work for a company that has the reputation of being the best, your customers will expect you to assume responsibility for everything associated with your product, even if the product is not at fault. They expect this support because you are the best and the best do those things.

Perceptions are important because they set the customer's **level of expectation.** A level of expectation is what the customer expects will happen in a given situation. The higher the level of expectation, the costlier it will be to resolve the issue or make a sale.

In order to be successful as a company, we must strive to set the expectation level of our customers at a reasonable level. We accomplish this by not overstating the performance and reliability of our products. We establish warranty guidelines and adhere to them on a consistent basis. We also do not promise more than we can deliver.

Another critical factor in dealing with perception is knowing what is currently being done in your industry and other comparable industries. Since perception is formed by multiple experiences, you must perform equal or better to other companies in your area or run the risk of being the target of a negative perception. In order to stay current with your competition, you must.....

Know What's Going On Down the Street!

You are a part of a company, or own a company, that is part of an entire industry. It may be a small industry, producing a single specialized product, or a very broad industry such as home improvement products. No matter what kind of business you are in you must do one very important thing to stay successful and competitive. You must know what you competition every day!

It is impossible to be competitive without knowing what your competition is doing. From the customer service side, you need to know warranty and service procedures at other businesses in your area. You should know their customer service policies and guidelines. You should find out what they're doing to make their customers happy. Are they introducing a new service or product? Do they do something you don't? Have they changed their image?

One sure-fire way to fail is to act like you are in a shell and can't learn from your competition. Rest assured that they are looking at what you're doing! Implement a new and successful service and your competition will soon be offering the same service, or an improved version. If you don't know what they are doing you cannot change your business to keep current and competitive.

As customer service professionals, it is worth your time to visit your competition and evaluate what they are doing to serve their customers. What makes you feel good when you go someplace else? What makes you uneasy? Pick apart what they do and identify any differences between them and you. What can you do to implement some of the good things? What can you do to eliminate some of the bad things? Learn from the mistakes of others. It's cheaper and faster than making the same mistakes yourself!

Believing In Yourself & Your Company

Back in the sixties there was all this talk about machines replacing human beings. In many applications that has, and is continuing, to happen. It may be depressing to think about, but for customer service people there is a bright spot!

Have you ever tried to get a problem resolved through an automated operator system? It is very frustrating and not at all customer friendly! I do not think we will ever see the day where customer service people will be replaced by machines. Why? One very special quality that we all have. The ability to think and make emotional decisions.

When we interviewed for the jobs we now hold, part of the interview process evaluated our ability to communicate and think for ourselves. The ability to think for ourselves is the very reason we were chosen for the jobs we do on a daily basis!

The ability to think enables us to treat each situation as it really is, a situation with unique aspects that must be considered before a decision is made.

I may lose a few people here but I do not believe a customer service person can be effective if he or she follows one specific course of action whenever a problem comes up. When someone asks we for a company policy that will cover every problem and provide a generic solution, I ask them if they are in the right line of work.

Customer service means thinking. Thinking about how to best serve he customer. Thinking about what is best for the customer and the company. Thinking about special circumstances that may require special actions on you part. Thinking about what you can do to keep that customer coming back again and again.

Customer service also means believing in your skills and your company. You cannot expect to satisfy your customer when you don't believe in what you are saying and doing. Customers will pick up on it. They will sense the lack of commitment. Believe me, they will see it. In order to effectively serve your customers, you must believe in what you're doing.

Believing means understanding your company's products and services. It means knowing the company procedures and guidelines and believing they are fair and applied consistently. It also means taking responsibility for making problems with these rules and procedures known.

Rules and regulations are subject to change as our businesses adapt to a changing environment. What was fair 10 years ago may be unfair now. What worked before may not work now. Because of this, rules and policy must change with the times.

Change occurs only when there are complaints and these complaints are made available to those that make the rules and regulations.

Develop an Escalation Procedure

You are going to run into situations where you are just not going to be able to resolve the issues at hand. This could be due to a number of reasons. The customer could be unreasonable, you don't have the information the customer requires, the customer is asking for something that you can't provide, or your personality just conflicts with the personality of the other party. Whatever the reason, you must have a plan in place to deal with these situations.

The plan you need to have is called an **escalation procedure.** An escalation procedure is a plan that lets you know who you should involve in the situation when you reach a stagnant point. By knowing whom to contact, you can seamlessly move the situation to the next level quickly and easily.

The first step in an escalation procedure is to establish a chain of command. This will give you the person to involve when the customer asks to speak to someone at the next level. Who will take those calls or talk to those customers? What about service issues? Who will respond to those problems? Think of other potential problems. Who will you escalate to for billing problems? Delivery problems? Try and think of all the possibilities.

When you have these situations identified, sit down with your company management and put together a plan for escalating trouble issues. When you are finished, put the plan in writing so that all employees will have a clear understanding of who will be called for what reasons. You completed plan should look something like this:

Management	Mr. Smith	x259
Billing or credit	Mrs. Fedele	x236
Service	Mrs. Kaufmann	x212
Delivery	Mr. Jones	x223

You would continue until all contacts have been listed. Everyone on the list should have a clear understanding of his or her responsibilities. They must be made aware that they will be the contact person for their department.

When you use you escalation procedure, you should always brief the contact person on the particular problem you are having before transferring the call or introducing the person to the customer. Try and provide all pertinent information so that the person will know if the customer is changing his or her story to get a better resolution. You may not believe this, but customers have been known to leave out some bits of information when talking to someone new to the conversation!

If you are going to involve someone new to resolve the problem, give the name of the person and, if you are talking on the phone with the customer, the persons phone number. This way, if you should get disconnected during the transfer, the customer will no who to contact in the future.

You may also escalate customers to other people in your own department that are at your same level. Sometimes all that is needed is a different face or voice to sooth the customer and resolve the issue. In some cases, you may wish to switch from a male to a female and vice versa. The entire object is to get the customer calmed down and responsive to what it is you are trying to accomplish.

If you have system of record keeping that supports notes and comments, it is a good idea to keep track of who the customer has talked with or contacted. If you have this information available, you can avoid sending the customer back to someone that he or she has already spoken with.

Sending a customer back to someone they have already talked with is a sure-fire way to increase customer frustration and anger.

There is one last issue regarding escalation that you must agree with and understand if you want to be effective in customer service. You must not take it personally, or consider yourself as having failed, if you have to escalate a problem. If you can't resolve it and someone else does, it just means that your approach or personality clashed with the customer. There will be instances where you will resolve a situation that the other person couldn't. It is not possible to make everyone happy all the time. Don't take it personal. You may also find yourself picking up new techniques and methods for dealing with certain kinds of people and problems.

If you make a mistake, learn from it. If you have to escalate to someone else, don't take it personally. It is better to escalate a problem than to keep trying and possibly lose a customer. If you refuse to escalate, and you fail to solve a problem, then you should take it personally. Think of your escalation plan as a tool for you to use to better serve your customers. If you look at it in that context, you will be more inclined to use it!

Follow-Up Is the Key

Do you want to see your customer satisfaction levels go through the roof? If you do, read and reread the following paragraphs. It's all common sense but most businesses don't do it like they should!

Many people and businesses are good at resolving issues and making the customer happy. Those are critical skills that are necessary to maintain a profitable business. The key to customer satisfaction is taking those skills one step further. That step is called follow-up.

Follow-up means contacting the customer a few days, or weeks, later to find out if everything is all right. Are they still having problems or is everything okay now? Were they satisfied with the way they were treated? Is there anything that could have been done better? All these questions provide you with the information you need to make changes and improve your operation. Some additional questions might be:

Did our representatives treat you with courtesy?

Were your complaints addressed in a timely manner?

On a scale of 1 - 10, how would you rate your experience?

How can we better serve you in the future?

These questions, and many others, will provide you with invaluable feedback about your company.

You may ask yourself why we are talking about surveys in a publication designed for front-line service people. The answer is that these surveys contain information that all customer service people need to be aware of. Front-line people or other employees can take these surveys as informal verbal surveys. While the most honest answers will tend to come from mailed in surveys, any information gathered by any source can be valuable in shaping your policies and operation.

Follow-up can also be viewed as getting a second chance. As previously discussed, customers will often just stop doing business with you without ever telling you why. They may be intimidated by the employees or just embarrassed to complain. A follow-up survey allows your customer to tell you what they think in a non-confrontational manner. Because of this, mail in surveys will tend to be more accurate than face to face verbal surveys.

To increase the accuracy of these surveys, the follow-up survey should be done within a relatively short time after the original problem. This is because we tend to forget details as time goes on. For the most accurate results, get the follow-up done quickly. This also reduces the time it takes to resolve issues that may still exist.

I suggest that front-line people ask basic questions to every customer they deal with. A generic question like, "Was everything done to your satisfaction today? may be all that is required to get a customer to talk about a problem they had. The entire focus should be on getting the customer to communicate their thoughts and perceptions to you so that you can address these issues quickly and effectively.

One word of caution concerning follow-up questioning or surveys. You might not like what you hear! Asking customers for their opinions may open you to a barrage of criticism and anger. While this may be unpleasant, always keep in mind that this feedback will help you make the right changes to your company and keep your customers satisfied! The closer you get the less negative feedback you are going to hear.

A word of caution regarding customer feedback. Never stop asking the questions! It is easy to follow-up when things are not going right and you need the information. The problem starts when you correct the problems and feel everything is wonderful.

The inclination may be to stop asking for feedback and eliminate the cost of the surveys and manpower. Don't do it! Always remember that you competition is doing the same things as you are. When you make a change that works, they will do the same thing. Customer Service feedback surveys and follow-up keep you aware of how your customers are thinking about you every single day.

Be a Part of the Solution!

In every company there are two types of people, those that complain and those that become part of the solution. In order to be effective, you need to become part of the solution.

You have probably noticed the employee who constantly complains. They find fault with everything. This is wrong, that should be done better, problems are holding them back from true success! Every business has at least one of these employees. They are quick to point out a problem but are always missing from working out the solutions. These employees have a limited value to the company.

A valuable employee is an employee that recognizes a problem and takes steps to find a solution for it. You can easily recognize these employees, too. They are the ones asking a lot of questions and thinking about your answers.

When they run into a problem, they will present that problem to the company along with ideas on how to solve it. They become part of the group that is charged with fixing the problem.

A good employee also does not discriminate over job title or position in the company. They realize that the person who drives a truck may have more accurate information regarding deliveries than the President of the company.

As a front line employee, you have access to a wealth of information. That information is contained within the minds of your customers. If you assist someone with a problem, take the time to investigate the problem and create a solution. Find out what the customer thinks about the problem. Find out what they think should be done different. Find out what they think is being done well and what needs to be improved. Without this information, you could spend hours addressing something that is already working well and ignore the real problem!

There are no Non-Important Jobs!

One very common remark made by front line people is that their jobs are just not considered to be all that important. The people that make the difference are the managers and professional staff. Whiles it's true that management makes decisions and plans the future of the company, it must also be realized that everyone in the company has a position of importance. Let me illustrate this point for you.

Your company introduces a new product. Engineering worked out all the problems so it's going to be real reliable. Management did their homework and priced it right and advertised it properly. They know wait for the reaction of the customers.

What would happen if the person who stocks the shelves let that product sit in the stockroom? What if the driver that brings the product to you store made a wrong turn and got lost? What if the salespeople didn't read up on the new product and did not offer it to their customers?

Last, but not least, what would happen if empty boxes were left on the floor of the store blocking the product from the view of the customers?

Every one of these examples would significantly reduce the amount of product sold. The product is good, the pricing is good, but something prevented the customer from having access to the product.

What happens if the customer buys the product, waits for delivery, and the delivery person never shows up? How do you think this would effect customer satisfaction?

You must establish in everyone's mind, that customer satisfaction is a company effort. Everybody from the top down has a specific function in the customer service process. The entire process will only be as strong as it's weakest link.

We have talked about this before but it bears repeating. There is value to everyone's input. The delivery person may know more about delivery problems than anyone else in the company! The clerk in the warehouse may be able to tell you more about goods damaged in transit than any of the engineers. Don't shortchange yourself and your customers by discounting the value of everyone's knowledge. Make sure everyone feels that they are part of the process.

Conclusion

Today everyone has a vested interest in seeing his or her company improve customer satisfaction. From the President down to the janitor, if the company does not remain profitable, jobs will be lost.

Our customers extend a certain degree of faith in your company when they make a purchase. It is everyone's responsibility to assure that this faith is rewarded with a pleasant and rewarding experience. Our customers must be made to feel appreciated and needed when they make a purchase. Start to take your customers for granted and you start yourself on the road to failure.

As an individual, you owe it to yourself to become the very best at what you do. Customer Service is not the easiest job in the world. Just the opposite. Those people is customer service have some of the most difficult jobs in the company. In order to excel in these jobs, it is important to take advantage of everything that is at your fingertips.

Take the time to improve your current skills and learn new ones. Evaluate yourself openly and honestly. Develop your action plan and monitor your progress. Never stop learning. The skills you learn today will have a measurable impact on your performance tomorrow.

The last thought I would like to leave you with is to be proud to operate as a team. Customer Service is not an individual task. It is a group effort. In order to achieve the maximum level of customer satisfaction, every department in the company must learn how to work together.

Your Keys to Customer Satisfaction!

Always strive to exceed your customer's expectations!

Be friendly and upbeat!

Make the customer feel at ease.

Offer your assistance; don't wait to be asked!

Listen to what your customers are saying.

Treat others like you would like them to treat you!

Listen to what your customers are saying.

Make the customer feel respected and important!

Make the most of your first impression!

Ask the right questions.

Listen to the answers.

Make all your comments positive

Listen to what your customers are saying!!!

Offer multiple options for solutions.

Escalate, if necessary.

Follow-up after problem resolution.

Always watch what your competition is doing

Take steps to eliminate future problems.

Your Keys to Personal Improvement In Customer Service!

Be honest in your self-assessment.

Identify weak and strong areas and skills.

Develop an action plan.

Use resources available to you.

Take pride in your successes

Learn from your mistakes.

Don't take failure personally.

Re-evaluate goals and objectives often.

Monitor your progress.

Look at what others are doing to improve

Never stop trying to improve.

Never stop looking for a better way.

Always be part of the solution.

Pitfalls to Avoid!

Never say "We can't do better than this."

Never think of customers as an inconvenience or people to be tolerated.

Never fail to keep up with what the competition is doing.

Never stop following up and gathering survey data.

Never think your customers can't go somewhere else!

Never think that you know more than everyone else.

Don't let yourself think you can stop and rest. Your competition won't!

A Note To The Reader

It is sometimes difficult to change something that we have been doing for years. These things have become habits. They have become part of us and our personality. The first step toward change is the realization that something is wrong and must be changed.

Our minds have a natural opposition to change. Change takes us out of our "comfort zone" and we associate negativity towards that change. When we associate negativity, our minds fight our attempts at change.

A powerful weapon to fight change is to envision all the benefits we feel we will get if we successfully change our behavior. The benefits may be money, prestige, power, success, freedom, or whatever we envision. Concentrate on these positive benefits and associate these feelings with the proposed change. It will provide you with the incentive you may need when things get a little rough.

Don't try to change everything over night. Take things one at a time and do not get overburdened. Slow but steady change is longer lasting than massive "gotta do everything now" change.

Be aware that we all experience failure at one time or another. Consider failure as a learning experience. Learn from your mistakes and move forward. Don't get discouraged. If everything always worked out exactly as you planned life would not be very rewarding. Look at the big picture and never lose sight of your goals. Your goals will keep you motivated and primed for success.

One final note. If you do achieve your goals, that's wonderful! Create new and more exciting goals to take their place and do one more thing. Give something back. Help others learn what you have learned. Work with co-workers to achieve their goals. The rewarding feeling you will get will be a feeling that will be remembered long after your help is over!

Good Luck!

For more information on Customer Service Training, please go to:

http://www.infowhse.com

www.ingramcontent.com/pod-product-compliance
Lightning Source LLC
Chambersburg PA
CBHW051318170526
45166CB00002B/587